26 DAYS OF CHRISISMAS

ZAZULEAC WORLD

From the creator of the Viral
PRESIDENT DONALD CHRISTMAS WRAPPING PATTERN

Merry Christmas

ISBN:978-1-957988-31-3

Designed in the U.S.A.

Table of Contents:

Day 1

The Sleigh Hits the White House Lawn

Santa crash-landed near D.C.'s gate.

The president yelled, "He's early – but that's great!"

Fox aired it Live with flashing lights.

And elves were tackled by Secret Knights.

TOP SECRET

Day 2

Mar-a-Lago Snowstorm

Snow fell in Florida? Must be fake.

Unless it's Coca-Cola in a frosted milkshake.

Santa wore shades and a red bathing suit.

The president served hot cocoa with a legal dispute.

Day 3

North Pole News Conference

Santa held a press at the candy cane stand.

"Elves want PTO; this wasn't planned!"

The President yelled, "I'll fix it – they'll beg me soon!"

Then sold ElfCoin live on Fox at noon.

Day 4

CNBC Sleigh Market Crash

The elves rang the bell at the North Pole Exchange.

Stocks for hot cocoa got wildly strange.

Santa panicked, "My sleigh's losing speed!"

The President grinned, "Let's short reindeer feed."

Day 5

Elf-Onlyfans

An elf went viral on CandyFans Live,

Wearing just gumdrops and sleigh number five.

Santa yelled "DELETE!" from his peppermint throne,

While POTUS subscribed to his backup iPhone.

Day 6

Elves Hack Wall Street

The elves rerouted NASDAQ lights,
And launched NFTs of reindeer flights.
The President bought one shaped like his head,
Then tweeted, "SantaCoin's not dead!"

Day 7

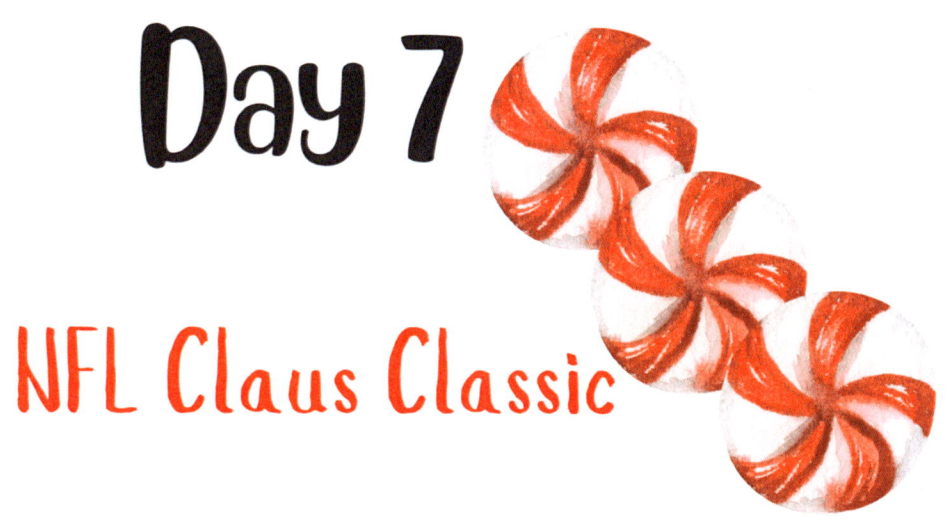

NFL Claus Classic

Santa punted from the fifty-yard line.

Rudolph moonwalked near the sideline sign.

The President threw candy like Brady throws.

Then flagged the ref for "Christmas prose."

Day 8

Sleigh Jam in Times Square

Rudolph froze at a red light flash,
While Santa did donuts at the Christmas bash.
The President wore lights like a blinking vest,
NFL called it, "His halftime best."

Day 9

TikTok Toy Trials

Santa made toys with dancing delight.

Then elves dropped spoilers on TikTok at night.

The President warned, "China's watching you spin!"

While Rudolph flossed with a smug little grin.

Day 10

Global Gift Inflation

The cost of gifts hit a record high,

Santa blamed elves and pumpkin pie.

The President held a Christmas press meet.

"Blame Canada. Or OPEC. Or sweets."

Day 11

Elf Data Breach in Silicon Valley

Santa's naughty list hit the net,
Elon offered a privacy bet.
The President blamed cookies and sued the Cloud,
Then yelled, "My sleigh's not hacker-allowed!"

Day 12

Holiday Hackers

Hackers stole the Nice List in digital bites,
Santa blamed Russia – The President said, "That's right!"

"Maybe it's China, or elves gone rogue,
Or just a hoax cooked up by Vogue."

Day 13

Mars Sleigh Test Fails

SpaceX invited Saint Nick to launch.

The sleigh combusted during cosmic brunch.

The President blamed it on alien spam.

"Elon, next time, build it in Birmingham!"

Day 14

U.N. Naughty List Leak

Santa leaked files at a closed-door session,
Elf surveillance caused global confession.
President Donald laughed loud in a MAGA hat
Said, "See? I told you the Claus was a rat!"

Day 15

Hanukkah with Heat

Santa spun dreidels over fire,
As elves debated kosher attire.
Donald the President fried latkes, oil ablaze,
And blamed CNN for the "Jewish phase."

Day 16

Rudolph's Resignation

Rudolph resigned from his Christmas post.

Citing "toxic glow bias" in a tearful toast.

President Donald tweeted, "He's weak – not bright at all."

Santa replied, "At least he shows up to the call!"

Day 17

Google Maps Glitch

Santa got lost in Kathmandu mist,
Google rerouted him to a pizza list.
The President called, "Use Apple instead!"
Santa replied, "That app's basically dead."

Day 18

Chaos in Canada

In Quebec, the sleigh hit a pothole with force.

Spilled syrup and gifts all over a horse.

Santa apologized in perfect French.

While the President grumbled from a hockey bench

Day 19

SANTA

Kremlin Christmas Card

Santa sent Putin a peace-sign wreath.
Got coal in return... and a gold-capped sheath.
The President called it "Cold War cheer."
While elves drank vodka and danced with deer.

Day 20

Berlin's Bratwurst Sleigh Race

Santa rode reindeer on Autobahn tracks,
Elves threw sausages from Santa's sacks.
The President judged with schnitzel in hand,
And declared, "That was MAGA-tastic, and grand!"

Day 21

Eiffel Elves in Paris Parade

Santa wore stripes and flew by baguettes.

Elves rode scooters with berets and pets.

The President sipped his wine with brie.

And said, "Santa's French. He agrees with me!"

Day 22

Beijing's Great Sleigh Wall

Santa was scanned by a QR sleigh code,

While drones played carols in Mandarin mode.

President Donald got flagged for "ideological snow."

Then ate dumplings on a censored show.

Day 23

Dubai's Holiday Flex

Santa arrived in a luxurious sleigh,

Elves wore diamonds and oil-slick gray.

President D rode a falcon through perfume mist,

And trademarked "Shariah Claus" with a twist.

Day 24

Christmas at the Border

Santa got stopped by a snow patrol.

Elves detained in a candy parole.

President Donald T built a snow wall, "10 feet tall."

And claimed, "Mexico's paying — that's all."

Day 25

Christmas in Times Square

Santa flew low through neon and cheer,
Tossing gifts to every ear.
The President waved flags from a golden car,
Then claimed, "This Christmas – my best by far!"

Day 26

Boxing Day Blowback

Santa vanished with a candy grin,
Left behind just a note, whisky, and gin.
The President trademarked Claus and Sleigh Delight.
Launched "Trumpmas™"–for freedom's right.